The Shidduch Handbook

for
Parents and Singles

Julie Joanes

About the author:

JULIE JOANES is a lawyer and a shadchanit. She grew up in Southern California and made aliyah in 2009. She now lives in Telzstone with her husband and children.

Written by Julie Joanes

Design and layout: Catherine Julia
Cover illustration: Alexandre Falcao

ISBN: 9798850041519

Copyright 2023 © Julie Joanes
All rights reserved

Dedication:

Before getting my feet wet, I had no idea how time-consuming it is to be a professional shadchanit. This book is dedicated to my children, whose needs sometimes come after those of my singles. Nevertheless, they continue to urge me on, often coming up with their own great shidduch suggestions. And of course, this book is dedicated to my biggest supporter: my shidduch, my husband. He gives me sound advice to pass along and is always eager to help the cause.

Table of contents

	Introduction	5
CHAPTER ONE	Are You Ready?	7
CHAPTER TWO	Making Inquiries	13
CHAPTER THREE	The First Date	17
CHAPTER FOUR	After the First Date	21
CHAPTER FIVE	General Dating Advice	25
CHAPTER SIX	The Evolution of the Dating Process	31
CHAPTER SEVEN	When to Reevaluate Your Checklist	35
CHAPTER EIGHT	Money Issues	39
CHAPTER NINE	Important Topics to Discuss	43
CHAPTER TEN	Special Circumstances	45
CHAPTER ELEVEN	How to Get Engaged	47
CHAPTER TWELVE	After the Engagement	49
	Glossary	51
	Resources	53

Introduction

Whether you are the parent of a single in shidduchim or you are the single trying to find your zivug, this handbook will guide you through the entire shidduch process from beginning to end. To simplify matters, it is written as if the single is reading it, however the concepts are helpful to parents of singles as well. The handbook is geared toward the chareidi/yeshivish public, but more modern crowds can utilize many of the concepts explained herein. As a shadchanit, I hear the same questions over and over again. This handbook was born out of a necessity to provide comprehensive and detailed coverage of every aspect of the shidduch process in a succinct format.

Before you start shidduchim, ask yourself one question:

Are you ready to make room for another person in your life?

No one is perfect so you need to be prepared to accept both the good and the not so good that your future spouse will bring into your marriage. If you are ready, keep reading!

These guidelines outline the essentials needed to successfully navigate the parsha of shidduchim. **No matter what, everyone must realize that shidduchim is ONLY in the hands of Hashem.** We must do our proper hishtadlus and this is the purpose of these guidelines. If you follow these guidelines, you will be doing your proper hishtadlus to find your zivug.

Throughout the parsha of shidduchim, you must daven to Hashem for siyata d'shmaya and have emuna that the right one will appear at the right time. Rebbetzin Spetner advises the parents of a child in shidduchim to learn emuna for five minutes everyday throughout the process. If a shidduch does not work out or someone rejects you, say "boruch Hashem!" because you were saved from the hassle of continuing to spend time and effort on a person who is not your bashert! The goal is not to get everyone to say "yes." The goal is to find your predestined soulmate.

CHAPTER ONE

Are You Ready?

The parsha of shidduchim is inherently full of myriad emotions: excitement, nervousness, disappointment, anticipation, giddiness, frustration, rejection, joy, and relief, to name a few. The question of whether or not you are ready to start shidduchim is one you should discuss with your parents, older siblings, married friends/relatives, and your close mentors/Rabbi/Rebbetzin. Once you start, you can always take breaks, but you should be prepared to marry the first person you date if everything lines up.

I have heard many stories of people who dated dozens of people and when they reflect back, they think the ones who were suggested first were actually the closest to their ideal match. Unfortunately, they decided not to continue dating one of the first people because they thought they are only starting out and perhaps there is someone out there who is a bit smarter, prettier, wealthier, taller, thinner, and on and on and on... Many older singles can relate to this storyline.

Once you Decide to Start

Once you decide to start shidduchim, you will need to do the dor yeshorim blood test to check for genetic compatibility. You can find out all the information about dor yeshorim from their website at: https://doryeshorim.org/. It generally takes three months to get the results so make sure to take care of this early in the process so you do not have to pay extra to expedite the results during dating.

In addition to dor yeshorim, you need a shidduch resume. The shidduch resume has all of your basic biographical information to give a superficial picture of who you are and your family background. A typical shidduch resume has the following information:

- Name
- Age (best to put date of birth which does not change with time)
- Location (you can also include other places you have lived for significant periods)
- Father's name and occupation
- Mother's name (and maiden name) and occupation
- Where you work or where you currently learn
- Schools you have attended
- Siblings' information (names, spouses, occupations, locations, ages, if they have children)
- References names and phone numbers (neighbors, friends, Rebbeim, teachers, family friends)

Some people also include a bit about the person's hashkafa and personality and what he is looking for in a spouse. People spend a good amount of time writing this section of their resume so it truly reflects who they are and what they want. If you receive a resume, read this carefully because it usually reflects the essence of the person accurately.

Regarding references, you can just put two or three and then if necessary, provide more later on. Many people do not want their neighbors and Rebbeim getting called constantly about a shidduch prospect that has little or no potential.

Shidduch Photos

The topic of shidduch photos is one fraught with controversy. On the one hand, a photo gives a general idea of what a person looks like and helps you avoid going out on a date if the other person's looks are completely not what you consider attractive. **On the other hand, a photo is a one-dimensional image which does not at all capture the person's energy or personality and sometimes, it does not even look like the person anyway!** Personally, I am against photos. If there is something particular about a person's looks that may concern you, try to find out about it in another way. Also, a photo may give one impression about the subject's personality which is completely untrue and you may have preconceived notions about the other's pnimius which affect your ability to have a fair and open dating experience. For example, you might think the boy looks overly serious in his photo, so you will go into the first date with that expectation, and as a result, you may subconsciously be "testing" him on the date to see if he is in fact overly serious. This can skew the dating process. Everyone should enter a first date with an open mind.

Insider's Tip: One main concern, usually of boys, is that girls are not overweight. There are subtle ways to find out if a girl is overweight without seeing her photo. For example, you can ask these questions to her references:

- "What does she do for exercise and keeping fit?"
- "Is a healthy lifestyle important to her?"
- "Can you describe what she looks like?"
- "Would you say she is on the heavier side?"
- "He is thin and athletic and looking for the same in a girl. Would you say they are the same?"

There are plenty of shidduch stories where one side said no or wanted to say no based solely on the photo and they ended up getting married. There are also instances where the mother of the boy decided, based on the photo of the girl, that she is not the boy's physical type, but they ended up getting married. If you are just starting out in shidduchim, try it without photos and see how it goes.

Unfortunately, many people will not agree to a first date without seeing a photo. So if you are going to send shidduch photos, make sure they are good quality. Also, you might as well send an up close headshot as well as a full-length photo, since the person requesting a photo presumably wants to see both views.

Here are tips for shidduch photos:

- Look at the camera! Many people send photos of their profile (side view of the face) or looking down. Look straight into the camera.
- Smile! People want to marry someone who is happy. Even if you have more of a serious personality, at least smile a bit in your photo.
- Dress normally, meaning not too fancy but not too casual either. Dress how you would dress for the date. You do not want to send a photo from a simcha where you are all "done up" and then the boy expects that very fancy look and is disappointed. Conversely, you do not want your shidduch photo to be shlumpy, no matter how much you love your sweatshirt.
- Look like yourself. For example, if you usually wear glasses, wear glasses in your photo.
- Try to show your true self, not the photo of someone who would attract the type you want. For example, if you are a woman who wears short sleeves, you should wear short sleeves in your photo. There is no point in trying to trick someone into dating you. Your photo should represent YOU! If you have multiple earring holes, show the multiple piercings in the photo.

I once set up a girl with a lovely young man who looked very serious in his photos. I asked for a smiling photo and the boy's mother said she would try to find one but never was able to deliver one. The girl agreed to a date anyway. It turns out the boy suffered from a condition where his face was paralyzed, which they did not want to disclose before the first date.

In another instance, a boy could not produce a smiling photo. He said he does not take good smiling photos. The girl went out with him and after three months of dating, he tells her that he suffers from depression.

In retrospect, when the boy could not produce a smiling photo in both of these stories, they had reasons that could have come out during the inquiries/birurim process, but instead, the girls had to wait until the date to understand why a smiling photo was not produced.

Once you have your shidduch resume, you should reach out to ONE shadchan who your friends/family recommend. People often make the mistake of reaching out to numerous shadchanim all at once when starting shidduchim. They feel like they should cast a wide net and can filter through all the ideas that come pouring in from all angles. This is the wrong approach because each shadchan will put time and effort into getting to know you and sending you ideas. Then, if one shadchan sends you a suggestion, you might say, "oh sorry we are busy with an idea from another shadchan."

While this is an inevitable part of the process, you are likely to get the most ideas all at once when you first start out in shidduchim, as opposed to later on down the line. So do the shadchanim a favor: meet them one at a time and take their suggestions one at a time to show that you are giving serious consideration to each one. And remember–Hashem will send the right one at the right time, through the right shaliach.

Insider's Tip: Don't ask the shadchan why he suggested a particular person. This is offensive and happens all too often. There is obviously a reason (or usually, many reasons), why a suggestion is made, no matter how random it seems. Sometimes, couples get married and people think "wow, I never would have thought of putting them together!" Hashem puts the ideas into our heads and we do our best to make thoughtful suggestions. If you receive a suggestion that seems like a mismatch, simply remind the shadchan what you are looking for that is not evident on this person's resume.

Once a shadchan sends you a resume that looks like it could be a good idea, you have a couple options. You can tell the shadchan to send your resume to the other side to see if they also think it has potential. This saves you time and effort if the other side gives a quick "no" based on something on the resume or the photo. Alternatively, you can tell the shadchan not to send your resume until you make a few preliminary phone calls to investigate whether this suggestion seems to be on target. This option will take more time and effort on your part because it might result in a quick "no" anyway from the other side, but it will save your references from getting called unnecessarily.

Some people prefer that the boy's side gives a "yes" before the girl's side starts making calls. Speak to the shadchan about which option works best for you.

I once worked with the mother of a yeshivish learning boy. I did not know her well but I knew a number of girls who I thought could be matim. The boy's mother preferred that I did not send her son's resume to the girl's side until she gave me the green light. So I gave her a few names of wonderful girls, some of whom I personally knew very well. She dismissed the names rather quickly, without asking for much information about them. To be honest, many of the girls' names she had heard before and determined they were not matim for her son. To my delight, there was an engagement announcement six months later of her son with one of the girls I had suggested! B"H! When I saw her at the erusin, she said "oh Julie, I didn't realize you know the girl's side so well." Apparently I was not the only shadchanit who suggested that shidduch, but she very quickly dismissed my suggestion, while, later on, deciding it was a match. I wonder if I would have sent her son's resume to the girl's side and the girl's side liked it, perhaps I could have encouraged the boy's side to give it more careful consideration six months prior.

CHAPTER TWO

Making Inquiries

After you see the other person's shidduch resume and the other side sees yours and both sides feel there is potential, then the inquiries begin. This is called "birurim" in Hebrew. Sometimes the boy makes inquiries first and sometimes both sides make them simultaneously. **The most important thing to keep in mind is that you are not inquiring whether this is a good person, you are inquiring whether this is a good match for *you*.**

Like on a food's ingredient list where the first ingredient listed has the most content in the food, the same is true when someone gives a list of middos describing someone. So if you ask a boy's roommate to tell you about his most outstanding middos, listen carefully to the first three mentioned because those encapsulate a larger part of the person than the ones mentioned at the bottom of the list. The same is true when someone writes on his resume about himself and what he is looking for in a spouse. The top of the list carries more weight than the bottom.

Do not be afraid to ask very specific questions and it is always good practice to prepare your questions ahead of time. For example, instead of asking "does she like to do chesed?" you can ask "can you give me examples of chesed activities she participates in?"

You do not need to know everything about the person before agreeing to a date. The basics you need to find out are: if the two singles are similar hashkafically and if there are any specific preferences that need to match up (preferred language, physical features, etc.) Many times people think they need a certain personality type and they end up with someone who is the opposite. For example, a person who is very outgoing might feel she needs someone even more outgoing, but she ends up marrying someone more on the quiet side. Therefore, I always encourage people not to discount someone who has very good middos and many character traits that match up if personality seems not to be an exact fit before the first date. Just because someone is described as quiet or reserved does not mean he is awkward or unable to hold a lively conversation, especially after he warms up.

Here is a list of questions you may want to ask during your inquiries:

- How do you know the person? For how long have you known him?
- Does he plan to stay in learning long-term?
- What are his most outstanding middos?
- Does he smoke?
- We all need to work on things. What are some areas she needs to work on?
- Would he ever consider moving back to America?
- How does he plan to make a living?
- Is he academically intelligent? Is he street smart?
- Is the family baal teshuva, Ashkenazi, Sefardi, gerim?
- Is she the more put together/fancy type or more casual in her dress?
- How does he spend bein hazmanim?
- If he suffered a trauma (loss of a parent/sibling, lo aleinu), did he go to therapy?
- Was there a broken engagement?
- Is he healthy physically/mentally/emotionally?
- Is there any mental illness or genetic issue in the family?
- Do you know if he takes any medication?
- What does he do for fun?
- Is he more outgoing or reserved?
- Where does he want to live?
- Does he do any chesed activities? If yes, can you give an example?

Do not ask all of these questions to all the people you call. Choose a few questions for each reference. Many times the person's references report back to the family that someone called about their child and the conversation is given over to the family. I have heard numerous stories where a family said "no" to a shidduch suggestion based on the questions presented during birurim.

One mother of a boy asked me to ask the girl's side if the girl is likely to be the type to put her husband up on a pedestal. I happen to know the mother asked this on more than one occasion to other shadchanim, and perhaps she asked this every time she did birurim on her son's behalf. The girl's family did not pursue the shidduch and while I am not certain, I think this question put them off. To me, it shows the boy needs someone to put him up on a pedestal and is unable to get up there by himself.

Sometimes the shadchan knows the answers to these questions, but the references listed on the person's resume presumably know the person the best. That is why their names are on the resume!

Insider's Tip: Try to find a common connection who knows both singles or at least both families to see if it would be a compatible match. The families, to a certain extent, are marrying each other. Also, try to do a little investigative work and speak to people who are not listed on the resume who know the single or family from an "outsider's" perspective. However, keep in mind that if someone who knows both sides does not think it is a good idea, make sure there is a good reason. Just a "feeling" that it would not work is insufficient. Also if a third party says that the singles would not mesh well because of personality differences, I would not follow that person's advice if other things lined up. There are so many happily married couples out there whose common acquaintances would not have "seen it."

Once you have made sufficient inquiries and you feel the suggestion could be compatible, tell the shadchan you give a "yes." **Once you give a yes, you are *frozen* from pursuing other shidduch ideas, no matter how much more relevant they may seem than the current idea.** This is even true if a shidduch idea from the past resurfaces. When one side gives a yes, the other side should respond with a "yes" or "no" within one week. If the checking is taking more than one week, the shadchan should get involved to try to help move things along. It often happens that a person's references are difficult to reach. People are busy. In this case, the shadchan can have the references call the mother/father of the single. If one side gives a "no," there is no requirement to tell the shadchan the reason. It can help the shadchan search for a more appropriate match, but halachically, the person giving a "no" can simply say it is not matim/shayach and the shadchan should not push for an explanation.

If both sides give a yes, then they usually check for any genetic issues with dor yeshorim. Once the results come back all clear, the shadchan sets the couple up for the first date.

CHAPTER THREE

The First Date

First Date Logistics

Following the American model, if the boy drives, he can pick her up at her house and briefly meet her parents. In Israel, the couple can meet at the date location or sometimes the girl's parents or father will escort her to the date. The first date typically lasts between 1.5-2 hours. You should wear Shabbos clothes, including a hat and jacket in the chareidi circles. In the more open circles, discuss first date attire with the shadchan so both singles are on the same page.

Many people like to meet in a hotel lobby or cafe. Hotels are ideal because you are unlikely to see people you know there (except other singles on dates). Others like to walk and talk. Walking is great because it helps people open up. Discuss with your shadchan if you have any preferences. The shadchan sets up the logistics of the dates. In religious circles, you do not talk on the phone or text with each other, generally until the engagement. Some couples feel having a phone/texting relationship will help them become comfortable enough to get engaged, so then, by all means, they can communicate directly. If the couple communicates directly to set up dates, they should make sure to keep the shadchan informed regarding the dating progress and reach out with any questions or issues. On the first date, the boy offers to buy the girl a drink, even if she brought along her own water bottle. He should also buy himself a drink. Most couples do not get food until date 3 or later.

I set up a couple and the girl ordered a drink. The boy ordered tap water. When the time came to pay the bill, the boy did not offer to pay, so the girl paid herself. This was one major reason the girl said "no" to another date. Afterward, I asked the boy why he did not also get a drink and he said because he likes water. I had to explain to him that this made

17

the girl uncomfortable. When you take space in a restaurant, you should at least order a drink for both people sitting there, so she is not the only one drinking a purchased beverage. And of course, the boy (in this case he was 39 years old!) should pay for both drinks.

The purpose of the first date is to see if it is pleasant and enjoyable to be in the other person's company. **We are not looking for fireworks, chemistry, or any long-term projections of a successful marriage.**

First Date Topics to Discuss

The conversation on the first date should be somewhat superficial. Do not discuss anything controversial, but also try not to bore the person. Do not get into anything too deep in your personal lives. Be real, be comfortable, be yourself, and be spontaneous so the conversation flows rather than feeling like a KGB interrogation. Good first date topics include: work, camps attended, how one spends shabbos/holidays, hobbies/interests, travel stories/plans, and news/current events. Imagine you are talking to the person next to you on an airplane. You do not want to offend the other person on the first date with any strong opinions. Keep it pleasant, keep it simple, keep it surface-level.

Example questions:

- What do you usually do for Shabbos? Do you like to have guests/be a guest?
- Did you travel anywhere during the last chofesh? Where?
- What do you most/least enjoy about your work?
- Which subjects do you enjoy learning the most?
- If you could travel to any time period, which would you choose and why?

You want to ask open-ended questions, not "yes" or "no" questions as this helps the conversation flow. It is a good idea to prepare before the date a joke, a d'var Torah, or an interesting story to tell if there is a lull in the conversation. As the date is coming to a close, the boy should drive her home or ask the girl if she wants him to wait for her bus or escort her in a taxi and he will pay for the taxi (some girls prefer not to be seen waiting at a bus stop with a date). Discuss this with the shadchan ahead of time so there are no unpleasant surprises.

You can end the date by thanking the person and saying "have a great day/night/Shabbos." You do not want to say "see you later" or "we'll speak" or anything like that. Then, call the shadchan soon after the date finishes to share your thoughts. **Even if you are not sure whether or not you want to continue going out, it is appreciated when you call the shadchan within a few hours after the date finishes to update the shadchan regarding your initial impressions.** You are entitled to tell the shadchan that you want to make more reference phone calls or ask your Rav/parents/mentor for advice before deciding whether or not to continue dating this person.

Active listening

How you make others feel about themselves says a lot about you. Active listening is very important on a first date, on every date, and in any real relationship. It means you hear what the other person says, you say something in direct response to it, and then you ask a follow up question that is relevant and related to the other person's original statement. Instead of asking a question, you can also tell your own story or comment that is related to what the other person said. A question is good because it helps the conversation to continue flowing.

Here is a very simple example of active listening:

She says "I'm a madricha at ABC seminary."

He says "that must be a hard/interesting/fun job. You must be a really good people-person to do that. What's the best part of your job? What don't you like about it?"

Active listening shows you are interested in what she is saying and you want to hear more about what she has to say. Look at her resume for ideas about safe subjects to discuss (camp history, work history, schools, where she has lived, where her parents are from, etc.)

On the first date, you simply want to enjoy your time together. You do not need to find out any information or dig into the person's past. **The ONLY purpose of the first date is to see if you two enjoy each other's company.** If the date was basically pleasant and enjoyable, then it is customary to agree to a second date. (Note: If the only reason you do not want to go on another date is because you are not attracted to the person, you should still go on a second date, especially if the other person wants to continue. Otherwise, it is just plain insulting.)

CHAPTER FOUR

After the First Date

Use the dates to notice the middos of the other person. Pay attention to what the other person says and also what he does not say. These are things you should look out for during the dating process. For example, if the person talks a lot about his father, but never mentions his mother, there may be a reason.

What is important in a spouse:

- Kindness
- Understanding/empathy
- Desire to help/please the other (thoughtfulness)
- Easygoing/flexibility
- Physical attraction/chemistry
- Similar hashkafa
- How the person relates to money (sometimes it is actually better where one person is more generous and one is more thrifty, but to be somewhat on the same page with finances is important in marriage)

How can you find out these qualities?

- Does the person do chesed/volunteer/help around the house/yeshiva?
- If you tell a sad story, does the person react with empathy?
- How does the person treat the taxi driver/waiter/person behind you in line?

What is **not** important in a spouse:

- Shared hobbies/interests
- Shared musical preferences
- Whether you are an early bird or a night owl

- Height
- Age (My husband is 10 years older than I am. 10 years is the age gap limit recommended by the Lubavicher Rebbe zt"l)
- Personality (this is a common misconception! Just because you are attracted to extroverts, for example, does not mean your zivug is an extrovert. Everybody opens up over time.)
- Shared language (as long as you can communicate effectively, you do not need to have the same mother tongues. English is my husband's second language.)

Danger Signs:

- Anger (screaming at the cab driver/waiter). Anger does not have to be loud. It can look more like someone is disgruntled or very frustrated. For example, a couple goes to a hotel for a date but the hotel turns them away, saying they are not allowing any more couples to date that night. How does the person react? Does he get angry at the doorman? Does he harp on this rejection for the rest of the date?
- Lack of patience
- Rudeness
- Controlling behavior (for example, attempts to control who is in your circle of friends or attempts to control how you spend your money)
- Harsh/derogatory sarcasm
- Extreme stinginess (kids cost!!)

Once the dating gets serious, a good date question is "what makes you angry?" or "what makes you stressed out?"

In marriage, you will deal with new types of stress and most people after marriage at some point turn into crazy monsters. (Not forever, just momentarily!) The hormones associated with pregnancy and the sleepless nights after birth (for both spouses) seriously impact a person's emotional equilibrium. When both spouses are sleep-deprived and you add a screaming baby to the equation (plus laundry, dishes, yeshiva/work schedules, paying bills, and other commitments), it is a recipe for disaster. At times like these, it does not matter if you like walks in nature and he prefers a concert. What matters is whether your spouse will help you when you need help and not criticize you when you make mistakes. People who, by nature, are warm, sweet, and understanding will weather the storm successfully.

Should You Continue After the First Date?

After each date, get back to your shadchan as soon as possible even if it is just to say you need time to think. In any event, you should give an answer to the shadchan within 24 hours maximum, unless there are extenuating circumstances. This is not meant to pressure you, it is meant to be considerate of the other side. Of course, as the dating progresses, it is normal to take more time in between dates to see if it makes sense to continue.

After the first date, there is only one question to ask yourself in deciding whether or not to continue to a second date: **is this person pleasant?** If the answer is yes, you should continue onto another date. Many people do not act like themselves on the first date due to a variety of reasons (nervousness, lack of sleep the night before, too much coffee on the date, etc.) and it is common courtesy to agree to go for a second date. There are many, many couples out there where at least one of the people wanted to say no after the first date but were willing to try again and they ended up getting married. Also, it shows the shadchan that you are open, flexible, and easygoing, which are traits we appreciate in our singles!

If the other person gives a "yes" to a second date, but you feel like saying "no," you should say "yes" for the following reasons:

1 It is the right thing to do. Be a mensch.
2 You never know who he knows. You want to make a good impression. If he knows your zivug, he is more likely to recommend you.
3 Saying yes to a second date does not obligate you in any way going forward after the second date.

4 There are **so** many stories of couples who are happily married where one side wanted to say no after the first date but they gave it another try.
5 There were good things about the first date.
6 Most people are not completely themselves on a first date. They can be tired, nervous, anxious, or just not comfortable showing their true selves because you are a total stranger.
7 It is crucial to have absolute clarity when you say no, especially if the other side says yes (at any point in the dating process). In other words, you do not want to have regrets that you closed the door too soon.

As my mentor, Danielle Leiba, a long-time shadchanit in Ramat Beit Shemesh taught me: **when in doubt, go out!**

CHAPTER FIVE

General Dating Advice

A second date should be longer than the first date: about three hours. Once you have met the person twice, you should have a much better sense of the person's personality, hashkafa, family background, and future plans. If the second date was pleasant and enjoyable and you feel there is enough in common to continue, then you will obviously continue. If you heard something from the other person that makes you think it is not worth continuing, discuss it with a mentor, parent, or the shadchan directly. Occasionally, people believe there is a problem when in reality, there is none. Other times, there is such a clear discrepancy between the two singles that it does not make sense to continue. For example, if she wants to send her children to chareidi schools and he refuses to send them to chareidi schools.

One thing is certain: if you are going to give a "no," make sure you have absolute clarity on the issue. You do not want to give a "no" because of something that is a "gut feeling" or some ambiguity. Two of my recent shidduchim nearly did not continue because the girls wanted to say "no," but decided to give it another try and both couples ended up getting married. They simply needed more time to get to know the boy better.

One story is about a couple who went out for a nice first date. The girl moved to Israel when she was 5 and has first cousins who are very Israeli. She always imagined she would marry a man like herself: an Israeli-American born to chutznik parents. I met a lovely American young man who I thought could be matim. They went out once and after the first date, he wanted to see her again. She said he is not for her. He is too American. I did not actually need to push her for a second date because her mother is a shadchanit, so she pushed her! **She said the standard is that if the other one wants to go out again after the first date and**

there were no major issues, you should go out again, even if you think it is not going anywhere. *She also told her to make sure she gets to know him well enough that if she says "no" after the second date, she will have absolute clarity that it is the right decision. They went out and stayed out. The mother was waiting and waiting and waiting to hear. After five hours, the girl sent the mother a message that he would be driving her home from the date and she wanted her parents to meet him. The rest is history.*

The Role of Hadracha in Shidduch Dating

Hadracha is an underestimated aspect of the shidduch dating process. In this sense, "hadracha" means giving feedback to the shadchan, who in turn, gives feedback to the other single so he can improve the dating process. Many people mistakenly think the couple needs to click automatically and if they do not like each other as presented, then there is no future for them. This is completely false. **Hadracha helps the dating process along and allows both sides to bring out the parts of their personalities that are not shining through, which the other person wants to see.**

*I set up a couple and the girl had not dated much. After the second date, the girl said the boy is not very warm. I reported this back to the mother of the boy and she was shocked. She said out of her ten kids, he is the **most** warm. The boy reserved his emotions on the dates. He is not the type to put himself out there emotionally until he gets to know someone better. He gave a coolish impression. The example the girl gave was when she said her newborn nephew was hospitalized, the boy did not show any sympathy. I told this to the boy's side and I told the girl's side what the boy's mother had said about him being the warmest of her brood. I also encouraged the boy to show his warm side more on the third date. On the next date, he apologized for not saying anything sympathetic about her nephew. (He had explained that she mentioned it just as he was dropping her off at home and sort of in passing, so he felt like it was not the time to start a new conversation. He just said goodbye and left.) After the third date, the girl's side was upset with me that I*

CHAPTER FIVE General Dating Advice

had told the boy's side she felt he was not warm. They said this shidduch process is not smooth if you have to tell him what to say. I said this is exactly what shidduch dating is all about. She was missing his warmth so I encouraged him to bring it out, which he did.

Regarding hadracha, you should feel comfortable to speak openly to the shadchan, not only regarding what you like about the other person, but also about your reservations. If there is something you do not want the shadchan to relay, make sure to specify that, and a good shadchan will keep that information confidential. However, feedback is crucial to the dating process. If you tell the shadchan you want to see the boy be more manly, she should relay this to him and then on the next date, if he is still not manly enough, you will know he is not hiding it anywhere–it simply is not a part of his character. If, on the other hand, you want to see a more manly man, but you do not tell the shadchan, perhaps the boy who is manly has gotten feedback that he is too aggressive or loud so he has worked to not show that side of himself on dates.

We must all keep in mind that the purpose of shidduch dating is to find your zivug. So if your zivug is manly, that needs to come out on the dates. If the boy thinks no girl wants such a go-getter type of guy because that is what he heard from the last shidduch which did not work out, then he will never show his true self and possibly be blocking his zivug from seeing the real him. For some women this "manliness" is important. For other women, they are perfectly comfortable with someone more reserved, relaxed, and chilled. Everyone should be themselves on the dates, to the best of their abilities, and definitely give feedback to the shadchan to pass over to the other side if you feel you need something in a partner that is absent in the person you are dating.

I set up a couple and the girl felt she was not seeing the boy's "fun" side. She knew he was the adventurous type, enjoying camping, surfing, and other fun activities, but she was not getting that vibe on the dates. He appeared very "chilled," which does reflect his true personality. After she told me she wanted to see his fun side, I relayed that to him and he said, how can I show her if we are not actually camping or surfing? I suggested showing her photos of his recent camping trip. B"H they are now happily married.

How to Show your Best Self

The majority of people do not show their true selves on a first date. It does not mean they are hiding anything; it means it takes time for people to feel comfortable enough to express their inner identities. Sometimes it can take a few dates and sometimes it takes months. Unless the person is purposefully trying to hide something, after 10 or 12 dates, you should know the essence of a person. Usually it happens somewhere between dates 4 and 10 if both sides are being honest, open, and transparent.

If you find it hard to show yourself completely on the dates, one idea is to show the other person photos of you being your best self, as mentioned in the previous section. This allows the person to see you shine, without the need or pressure to actually shine on the date. You can also prepare for the date by thinking of stories which accentuate parts of your identity you find difficult to express in action. For example, if you want to show your fun side, but find yourself tense and nervous on the first few dates, prepare stories showing your fun, lighter side so the other person can see it exists.

How to Best Utilize the Shadchan

Remember, the shadchan is supposed to help you. Use him as a resource. Ask for advice. A good shadchan does not want to make a mismatch. We want to help people throughout the dating process and we have a lot of experience in this field so use us wisely! Many people are not aware that they do not need to provide an apology or a reason for saying "no". It may help the shadchan look for more compatible matches, but if the reason for saying no will not help him search for you, then no reason is necessary.

CHAPTER FIVE **General Dating Advice**

Do not forget to show appreciation to your shadchan. We work hard and we do not get paid by the hour. Most people who try to be a shadchan quit because the amount of time they spend far outweighs any financial compensation they receive. While this has neither become standard, nor even expected in our community, I have received both gifts and cash for my efforts on behalf of a single person when I did not make his shidduch and such gestures are greatly appreciated.

The more pleasant you are to work with, the more likely the shadchan will keep sending you ideas. We try to help everyone who comes our way, but our time is limited and we are absolutely inundated with singles so we naturally are more likely to help the people who are easygoing and pleasant rather than the difficult or very picky people. Also, please please please do not be shady or a liar. Many older singles either lie about their age or simply refuse to give it. Trust is a major component in shidduchim, and in marriage. If you lie to the shadchan about one thing, you might be lying about everything and we cannot recommend such a person (or a mother-in-law) for a shidduch.

When you first meet a shadchan, inquire as to when is the most convenient time to discuss shidduchim and the preferred mode of communication. Some shadchanim prefer to talk on the phone, others prefer e-mail, and others prefer WhatsApp. Calling me at 3:30pm on a Friday afternoon to see if I have any new suggestions for you is not a good idea, no matter how much you want to check it off your list of weekly chores before Shabbos. Also anything you send on WhatsApp, whether written or oral, can be forwarded to the wrong person. So I highly discourage sending anything that you prefer to remain confidential between you and the shadchan, unless it is deleted quickly thereafter.

CHAPTER SIX

The Evolution of the Dating Process

While the first date should feel somewhat superficial, the dating process is an evolution and the couple naturally either grows closer or further apart as the dates progress. Generally on the second date, the conversation should get a little more in-depth and more personal. If you are unsure whether it is appropriate to bring up a topic of conversation, better not to do it and ask the shadchan after the date if it is appropriate to discuss on the following date.

Usually on the third or fourth date, the couple begins to discuss hashkafa: where to send kids to school, what type of community to live in, tsnius standards, technology in the home, davening/learning schedules, etc. If a single is curious about something in the other single but is not sure whether or not to bring it up, I often suggest introducing the topic as it applies to the speaker. This leaves the door open for the other person to offer his or her opinions without being put on the spot directly. For example, if the boy is curious about the girl's tsnius standards, he can say "my sisters always complain about having to wear tights in the hot Israeli summers. It must be so hard sometimes." Then, he should listen to how the girl reacts in order to see where she herself is holding with this issue.

Try to combine having fun on the dates with seamlessly weaving in questions and conversations that reveal pertinent information about yourself and the other person. Some couples can have a wonderfully fun time together, but not cover any topics of importance in marriage. Other couples sit across the table from one another, shooting questions back and forth in an attempt to discover compatibility. The dates should be a combination of the two methods.

Here are a number of date ideas in Israel. I advise having the shadchan notify the other side about the agenda for the date ahead of time. This allows the person to dress appropriately (hiking clothes, a jacket, etc.) Usually the boy plans the dates.

Date Ideas

- Picnic in Mitzpe Yericho
- Mini Israel
- Walk by the Beach
- Zoo
- Aquarium
- Jeeping/ATVing
- Ziplining
- Ir David Tunnel Tours
- Monkey Park
- Ein Gedi Nachal Arugot with a Picnic
- Billiards
- Bowling
- Karting
- Ceramics
- Live Music in Kikar Musica
- Kayaking
- Science Museum
- Boat Ride
- Park Hayam Ashdod
- Park Paris Holon
- Ice Skating
- Bumper Cars
- Chocolate Factory in Kibbutz Tzuba
- Board Games/Dating Game
- Make a BBQ Together
- Botanical Gardens
- Gan Sacher/Cafe Gan Sipur (need a reservation)
- Jerusalem Rose Garden
- Park Anava in Modiin (boat rides)
- Ganei Yehoshua Ramat Gan (boat rides/bicycles)

CHAPTER SIX The Evolution of the Dating Process

- Tel Aviv Port (scooter rentals)
- Ashdod Tayelet and Mini Zoo
- Ramat Gan Safari/Zoo (need a car)
- Hertzliya Marina
- Netanya Tayelet
- Escape Room
- Babylon Park Jerusalem (arcades/bowling)
- Cafe Rimon in Mamilla and Teddy Park
- Paint Night on Canvas
- Cafe Lyon and Walk through Shuk

The shadchan is the only one talking to both sides simultaneously, letting you know where you stand with the one you are dating and at times sharing their perspective to facilitate relationship building. The shadchan is the "safe space" to share the euphoria your heart is radiating and the hesitations your brain is broadcasting. With each couple of dates, you should either feel that you have more and more in common and there is more potential to marry this person or the opposite. If you continue dating and you feel there is a plateau, then it is probably time to make a decision. At some point you will be ready to commit and you will be encouraged to close at the point you are sure. Some people know very quickly and for others it takes much longer. Patience and common sense are key. Also, an unbiased outsider like a dating coach can help guide you if you feel the relationship is stuck.

CHAPTER SEVEN

When to Reevaluate Your Checklist

I preface this section by apologizing in advance for offending anyone. My intention is only to help and guide you through shidduchim to the chuppah. Everybody has a dating checklist. Everyone wants someone with good middos, but others also want someone who is wealthy, beautiful, intelligent, from a certain type of family, from a certain yeshiva/seminary, the right height/age range, a certain career path (for both men and women), a specific ethnicity/culture, certain physical characteristics, and the list goes on and on and on.

In addition to all the abovementioned "requirements," many people also refuse to consider anyone whose parents are divorced, anyone who has a broken engagement, anyone who was adopted (even if the birth parents are Jewish), anyone with special needs siblings, and more. **Of course people need to match on many criteria, but sometimes singles need to reevaluate their dating checklist.** The longer you date, the shorter your checklist should become, but I have seen the opposite on far too many occasions.

I knew a great guy who was having trouble with shidduchim. He did not fit into any hashkafic box. He watched YouTube videos after work to relax and he worked as a social worker in a Jewish setting. The girls who were ok with his YouTube watching were not excited about his career as a social worker. Also there was at least one other issue of which I was aware. However, he was a good person, with good middos, spoke perfect English and Hebrew, was not bad looking, was intelligent, a great conversationalist, and very grateful for my assistance. He excitedly called to tell me he got engaged (not through me) when he was 29, but the excitement was short-lived as the engagement was called off the next day. Apparently there was a miscommunication regarding where to settle after marriage. After this experience, he told me he realized that from now on, he would only consider women whose parents live in Eretz Yisroel, women who would also work to support the family, and he would no longer compromise on a girl's look. He needed to be attracted to the photo or else he would not meet her. None of these conditions existed before his engagement, but now, not only does he have a broken engagement under his belt but he also has a longer checklist. I have not been able to get him on a date since.

On the other hand, I have had people contact me after dating for two years or more and tell me they are open to hearing suggestions of people who formerly would not have fit their requirements. For example, someone who only wanted an Ashkenazi is now open to a Sefardi. Someone who only wanted up to age 25 is now ok with up to age 29. Someone who only wanted a chutznik family is now open to an Israeli family.

When I first wrote this handbook, I wrote that when a girl is up to age 24 and a boy is up to age 26, the checklist should be at its longest, but still within reason. I advise people to have a list of "needs" and a separate list of "wants." Many people confuse the two. In the yeshivish world, once a girl hits 25 and a boy, 27, the checklist should be seriously shortened. If a single has been dating for five years or more, one can assume the pool of potential matches who satisfy the entire checklist has dramatically diminished. Of course, this applies to the frum from birth crowd, not baalei teshuva. With the frum from birth group, once the single becomes 30, the list should be reduced to 3 requirements. I suggest the following 3 points: similar hashkafa, physical attraction, and good middos. Parnassa, family history, cultural background, height, type of kippah, and basically any other criteria should be thrown out the window if you want to get married. **Once a single becomes 35, the ONLY factor should be middos.** If you meet someone with good middos, jump at the opportunity to start a family with someone with good middos! No one wants to admit this, but the goal at this point is not to find someone amazing and wonderful, like when you were younger. The goal when you are 35-plus is to find someone who is good enough so you can start building a family before it is too late.

CHAPTER SEVEN When to Reevaluate Your Checklist

During the writing of this handbook, however, I came across a very interesting piece of advice by Rav Avigdor Miller zt"l. He says a person should start to compromise on their checklist **from the very first shidduch**! When I think back to the shiduchim I was zoche to make, the vast majority of them did compromise on one or more points. Here are the real-life examples:

- She wanted an Israeli-American and ended up with a total American.
- He wanted a Breslov father-in-law with whom he could travel to Uman on Rosh Hashanah. He ended up with in-laws who are in-the-box American Modern Orthodox.
- She wanted an English speaker and ended up with a complete Israeli who speaks zero English. (The mechutanim cannot smoothly communicate with each other but the couple is beautiful!) Also, he smokes which is something she was against. However, he never smokes in the apartment and the mother-in-law told me she has never smelled smoke on him.
- She wanted a healthy family background like her own and her chosson's parents had a very nasty divorce.
- She wanted a black and white chareidi yeshiva guy with no smartphone like her father and she ended up with someone who wears colored shirts, did the army, and has a smartphone.
- She wanted someone loud and opinionated like her brothers (and herself) who could hold his own during feisty family debates and she ended up with a very chilled out, calm gentleman.
- He wanted someone thin, like himself, but at age 44, decided to go for someone a little chunky. He had never dated a girl who was not thin, but friends set them up. She's 35 and they have great chemistry and similar hashkafot b"H.

All but one of those singles were under 28 years old. I mention this to point out that it is not as if they were dating for two decades and felt they had to compromise or settle. They were open-minded daters and they all found their zivugim who looked a bit differently than they had imagined.

Some people are simply too picky. For example, I have encountered:

- A giyores who will not consider a ger. (She's 37 by the way).
- A woman divorced with a child who will not consider a man with a child.
- A 34-year-old woman who will not consider a man over age 36.
- A 40-year-old woman who will not consider a man over age 42.
- A seriously obese man (34 years old) who will not consider a heavy woman.
- A 65-year-old man who will not consider a woman over 35 years old.
- A 45-year-old woman who refuses to marry a divorced man.
- A Temani, baal teshuva 30 year old long-term learner who is 5'7" and refuses to consider a woman who is shorter than 5'10". The taller the better, he says.

People ignore the fact that the dating pool shrinks with time. It constantly amazes me how older singles seem to think their besheret has been hiding, waiting around for them. Once in a long while you hear of a story of an older single who presumably "got what he was waiting for all those years" but this is simply not the reality for 99% of the singles over 35 out there.

I have worked with a number of older men (into their 60s) who are still waiting for a woman who can have biological children. The best way to reevaluate whether your checklist is reasonable given your age and other circumstances is to ask an objective outsider. When looking in the mirror, most people see a face of reason. This is why it is crucial to get an outsider's opinion.

I met a lovely woman in her early thirties. She was smart, pretty, bilingual, worldly, came from a good family, solid in her hashkafa, had a great job, and seemed an all around great catch. But she had been dating for a decade and was still single. Also, it seemed as if she had been suggested to almost every eligible man out there and there was simply no one left. I wanted to know if she was particularly picky and perhaps this was holding her back from finding her zivug. I asked her what she now would consider in a man that, when she was younger, she would not have considered. She told me one thing: a younger man. I wish her the best of luck.

CHAPTER EIGHT

Money Issues

There is no "one way" to handle the money question in shidduchim. For couples where the boy is in a top, mainstream yeshiva and will sit and learn for the long term, usually his side asks for enough money to give a down payment on an apartment, plus they look for a girl with a good job to cover mortgage payments. This can reach up to 800,000nis in some circles. And yes, girls actually exist who pay this amount. The rationale behind this arrangement is that if the boy is really going to be able to sit and learn without the pressure to provide financially for his wife, children, and home needs, the money will need to be provided from somewhere. The roshei yeshiva set certain standards for their talmidim because they see the boys who are comfortably situated after marriage are more successful in their plans for long-term learning.

However, there are no set rules and each family has a different financial situation. There are also boys who hope to learn long term and they do not ask for any money from the girl's side. They plan to figure it out on their own and they do! Where the boy is studying or working, generally the parents split paying for the wedding expenses and help setting up the apartment but then the couple is on their own.

Many parents are prepared to financially help the new couple, but do not have a set number that they expect the other side to provide. Generally, the girl's side pays for the engagement party and each side pays for half of the wedding expenses. Of course this can be arranged differently between the families. Some parents split the engagement party and Shabbos Chattan and Shabbos sheva brachos. In America, the girl's side pays for more of the wedding. Some people follow the opinion that the boy's side pays for FLOPS: flowers, liquor, orchestra, photography, and sheitle and the girl's side pays for all the other wedding expenses. Generally the girl's side pays for setting up the apartment with furniture, appliances, and the rest of the apartment interior. Some parents decide to go 50-50 on everything.

If you have a specific expectation, it is crucial you tell the shadchan as early as possible during the shidduch process. In fact, even if you do not have a specific expectation, it is helpful to discuss your financial expectations at the beginning of working with the shadchan so you will get appropriate suggestions. It is truly heartbreaking when an engagement is broken off because of misunderstandings involving money and I have seen it happen all too often.

When I first started working as a shadchanit, I set up a 24 year old girl with a 26 year old boy. He was in full-time learning, but planned to go to Machon Lev the following year to earn a degree. She comes from a family of 11 children, her father is an avreich and her mother is a homemaker. She had a steady job, but nothing fancy or with a particularly high earning potential. She needed a husband who would also work, especially after the first year. I knew the girl's side could not contribute much, except for the engagement party, a simple wedding, and simple apartment setup. The boy's side never mentioned money to me so I incorrectly assumed they had no demands. After the first date, both singles had a nice time and wanted to continue. That is when the boy's mother informed me that they are asking for 350,000nis for a down payment for an apartment. We were both shocked. I was shocked she had not told me this before and she was shocked I did not know "what all the other shadchanim know about her family demands." The girl's side said they could pay that amount in monthly payments over the course of 15 years. The boy's mother refused the offer, but said they should continue dating to see where it goes. I said I will absolutely not send a girl out with someone under these circumstances. The girl's side agreed with me and that was that. Both are still single, nearly two years later.

After that experience, I learned to ask upfront if there are any specific financial demands or expectations. You should have this discussion with your shadchan sometime before the singles meet to avoid any unexpected surprises and disappointments. Here is a list of specific points to discuss:

- How will expenses be divided for the:
    - Engagement party (some couples opt out of this)
    - Wedding
    - Apartment rental/down payment/mortgage
    - Apartment furnishings/appliances
    - Living expenses like food and utilities for the first year and beyond

CHAPTER NINE

Important Topics to Discuss

Some couples have such an easy, enjoyable dating experience, they forget to discuss very important topics during the dating process. One of these topics is family planning. Just because both people are religious, does not necessarily mean they share the same values when it comes to using birth control. Other topics that the couple should discuss before getting engaged are: where to live after marriage, how long the engagement should be, any potential health issues, and if there are any school/career plans already in the works for the future.

I set up a couple who dated for over three months. The boy was ready to get engaged after about six dates but the girl needed more time. They went on over a dozen dates and had spent many hours together. On the night of the engagement, the couple went back to the girl's home for a l'chaim. Mazal tov! At the l'chaim, the girl's mother started discussing possible wedding dates. They were engaged a couple weeks before Pesach. This is when the boy disclosed that he had spent the last two years applying to a special programming training for a large corporation overseas and if he was accepted, he would be basically away and very busy for a four-month period, from May to August. He would not be able to see his kallah, but only speak to her on the phone. Then, in September come the chagim so they were looking at a wedding in October at the earliest. This shocked everyone, including me! It was like he dropped a bomb. The girl's side was hoping for a wedding in June. The boy's side assumed the girl would accommodate his schedule. He should have mentioned this during one of their many dates.

If you have any plans for the future, make sure you share them with the person you are hoping to marry before the engagement. Never assume the other person will automatically accommodate future plans to which you have already committed, but have failed to disclose.

CHAPTER TEN

Special Circumstances

Hashem made every individual special, but some people have **very special** circumstances in shidduchim which necessitate a more open approach. I have worked with a single who is blind, two women born without a uterus, a bipolar young lady (and her siblings), men with asperger's, a schizophrenic, families with multiple special needs siblings, and of course more mild situations like people with ADHD and unique family circumstances (i.e. one frum parent, one not). Most people who fall into one of these categories realize they need to be more open in who they will consider as a shidduch, but not all of them realize this and it is certainly slowing down the shidduch process. **If you have a special circumstance, be open!** I am not saying you should settle, but there is a long way to go from the first date to the engagement. **People with special circumstances should say "yes" to a lot more first dates than they would if there were no special circumstances in the picture.**

CHAPTER ELEVEN

How to Get Engaged

Generally, one person is ready to get engaged before the other. Usually the other person just needs a few more dates so give him time and space and hang tight. **If it is right, it will happen at the right time.** Once both sides have told the shadchan they are ready to get engaged, the boy should plan a special time and place to propose on the next date, unless the girl wants to be surprised and not know when it is going to happen. Then, he will propose on one of the next dates, but does not need to say which one. I encourage both sides to write a note to the other side saying why they are so excited to be getting engaged. Highlight what you like about the person and give it to him at the engagement. This is a very special keepsake that you can hold onto forever to remember this exciting moment in your lives.

For the boy's side, when you are ready to propose, make sure to have friends or family set up the location for the engagement with flowers and perhaps chocolates, drinks, snacks, or whatever else you think she will enjoy. Make sure there will be someone there to take photos of the special moment. You can see engagement setup ideas here: https://simchaspot.com/. It is customary to give the girl jewelry at the time of the proposal. Some people do not give a ring as they view it as a goyish custom. In that case, you can give other jewelry.

Typically after the proposal, the couple goes straight to the girl's family to have a l'chaim with drinks and snacks. This usually includes both families and very close friends. In Israel, this is called the vort. In America, it is called a l'chaim. It is small and unofficial and the same day as the proposal. Then, usually within a week or two, there is a bigger party called the erusin. Here, the couple invites family and friends for the proper, official engagement party. Some mothers break the plate at the erusin and others do it at the wedding. Ask your Rav which is preferred, as there are halachic ramifications.

The erusin can be as big and fancy or small and simple as you like and some families skip on the erusin altogether. There are no set standards. You can host it in your living room or in a neighbor's apartment. Some people host the women in one apartment and the men in a neighbor's apartment if the space is too tight to have it in one place. You can prepare all the food yourself, with help from friends or you can get it catered, or partially catered. Other people go big and rent a hall with full-on catering, a band, and photographer. It feels like a mini wedding. The girl's side typically hosts (and pays for) the engagement party. The boy's side customarily sends a beautiful bouquet of flowers to put on display on the girl's side at the party. Ask friends and neighbors for advice and I am sure they will be more than happy to help celebrate this happy occasion!

In Israel, the custom is to pay the shadchan at the engagement party. Find out the rate beforehand so you can be prepared. In America, the custom is to pay at the wedding.

Remember: **no one is ever 100% ready!**

I remember at my wedding, my husband was coming toward me during the badeken to lower my veil and I had a mini panic attack. He looked different to me for some reason and I thought to myself, "oh no, what if I am about to make the biggest mistake of my life? Do I really know him well enough? What if I am wrong?" My yetzer hara was working overtime, but b"H I ignored it and am now happily married 16 years later.

We can never be completely certain about the other person, even though Cinderella would cause you to believe otherwise. We do our hishtadlus, we daven, and most of the time, b"H everything turns out just fine. Dating should be fun, exciting, but most importantly a vehicle to connect, earn each other's trust and respect, and eventually to feel at home so that "I" becomes "we."

CHAPTER TWELVE

After the Engagement

Mazal Tov! Now it is time to plan a wedding! Some engagements last four weeks and some last four months, or more. The wedding planning stage is extremely stressful as it involves the opinions of at least six people usually, and oftentimes even more (siblings, grandparents, friends, etc.). All the decisions to be made and how much to spend on everything can ruin a time that has the potential to be full of excitement and anticipation. **The most important thing during the engagement period is to maintain shalom between the chosson and kallah and the two families.** If a sticky question arises, seek daas Torah and do everything possible to keep the peace.

During the engagement period, it is customary to give the other side gifts. Here is a list of possible gift ideas. Most people do not give everything on this list.

For the chosson:

- Tallis (shabbos/everyday)
- Personalized tallis bag
- Set of shas
- Watch
- Kiddush cup
- Kittel
- Menorah (at Chanukah time)
- Esrog box (at Sukkos time)

For the kallah:

- Candlesticks
- Jewelry

- Siddur (personalized)
- Machzorim (personalized)
- Watch
- Jewelry for cheder yichud
- Flowers for shabbos

For the wedding night, line up someone to "house sit" your house because you do not want any uninvited guests to come to your house when they know it will be empty.

Mazal tov!

Glossary

Avreich: Full-time yeshiva learning man
Baalei teshuva: People who become more religious (lit. "masters of questions")
Badeken: Part of Jewish wedding ceremony where the groom veils the bride
Bein hazmanim: School vacation periods
Boruch Hashem (B"H): Thank G-d
Chagim: Holidays
Chareidi: Ultra-orthodox Jew
Cheder: Religious boys elementary school
Chesed: Act of giving
Chosson: Jewish groom
Chofesh: Vacation
Chutznik: Someone from outside Israel
D'var Torah: A word of Torah
Emuna: Faith
Erusin: Large engagement party
Frum: Religiously observant
Ger/giyores: A convert (m/f)
Hadracha: Advice
Hashkafa/hashkafos: Religious viewpoint(s)
Hishtadlus: Due diligence
Kallah: Jewish bride
L'chaim: Small affair celebrating an engagement in America
Lo aleinu: Phrase used to express "we should never know about these tragedies personally"
Madricha: Counselor
Matim: Relevant, appropriate
Mechutanim: Parents of one's son-in-law or daughter-in-law
Middah/middos: Character trait(s)

Parsha: Segment of time
Pnimius: Internality
Roshei Yeshiva: Heads of yeshiva
Shabbos chattan: The Shabbos before the wedding where the groom is honored in synagogue
Shadchan/Shadchanit: Male/female matchmaker
Shalom bayis counseling: Marriage counseling
Sheitle: Wig
Sheva brachas: Seven days of celebration following a Jewish wedding (lit. "seven blessings")
Shidduch: Soulmate
Shidduchim: The time period when one searches for his/her soulmate; soulmates
Siyata d'shmaya: Help from Heaven
Talmidim: Students
Tsnius: Modest dress
Vort: Small affair celebrating an engagement in Israel
Yeshiva: Religious Jewish school for men
Yetzer hara: Evil inclination
Zivug: Soulmate

Resources

(Some of these might be outdated. If you discover the number does not work or needs updating, please contact the author.)

Lerner Events
Full event production including dishes, tablecloth design, flowers, catering, waitstaff
Aryeh Lerner: 053-466-8669

Jerusalem Various Wedding Gemachim:
https://www.chesedmatch.org/israel/jerusalem/simcha-celebrations

Wedding gown and mother/sister of the bride/groom gemach
Ginzberg: Zichron Yaakov 12 (knissah alef), 02-537-2285
Klulot: Rechov Yaffo 38 (kuma bet), 02-623-1605
Adina Rom: Bayit Vegan, 02-642-0654
Sister of the Bride: Rechov Michal 9/3, 02-532-8935
Ringel: 02-537-1135
Ezrachi: Rechov Bayit Vegan 74, 02-641-2842 or 02-346-6262
Studio l'kallah: Sorotzkin 36, 02-538-6188
Shapiro: Yehuda Hamaccabi 18, 02-538-1878
Deganit: Rechovot, 08-945-7804
Yad Trudy: 30 Shaulson Sonia Turgeman, 02-651-9096
Preivert: 16 Admor M'Boyan, 02-651-9025, call for hours
Lerer: 16/1 Chai Taib, 02-651-9696, call for hours
Shalsheles: Pam Pogoda, 02-993-1326
Gemach: 14 Zerach Barnett, Har Nof, 02-651-2650
Hadassa Ost: Sorotzkin 49, 02-500-1207
Debbie Frohwein: Minchas Yitzchok 19, 02-538-6761
Tzurati: Shaarei Chesed, 02-624-2423
Har Nof: 02-651-2650

Froidbert: 02-651-9025
Porush: 02-571-2739
Telzstone: Lisa Askotzky 052-767-9215 or Yehudis Klinger 052-711-4919
Esther Ruchy Reichman: Hahanov 16, 02-563-1257

Bayit Vegan: https://www.ylakala.com/

Beit Shemesh Various Wedding Gemachim:
https://www.shemesh.co.il/en/directory/gemachim/_filter/~categories-15/-wedding-gemach?mode=list

Kallah classes and shalom bayis counseling
Elana Mizrahi: 053-429-3882, http://elanamizrahi.com/
Har Nof Kallah teachers: 02-651-4788 or 02-652-2633
Har Nof Chosson teachers: 02-652-3363
Ruchi Greenwald: 054-856-3750

Wedding Planners
Judy Bernstein: 02-651-9664
Baila: 02-537-3605

Halls
Bais Yisroel: 02-538-4534
Ulmei Nof (Bayit Vegan): 02-651-5999
Ulmei Gutnick (Beit Hadfus): 02-627-3444
Tamir (Mattersdorf): 02-572-4444 or 052-871-1181
Ulam Shalom (Bayit Vegan): 02-675-2222
Ulmei Palace (Talpiot): 02-678-3477
Yahalom Shebaketer (Talpiot): 02-679-2973
Ganei Yehuda (Talpiot): 02-672-2555
Beit Orah (Moshav Orah): 02-643-6251
Kol Mevasser (Mevasseret): 02-570-3097
Cheftzadi: 02-538-8107
Ulmei Maxim: 02-651-3058
Zvhill: 02-586-8313

Psagot Winery: 02-997-9333
Sakoya: 052-401-1152, sakoya-events.co.il
Olmaya Old City of Jerusalem: olmaya.co.il
Ein Hemed: ein-hemed.co.il
Hotel Yehuda: byh.co.il
Ramat Rachel: ramatrachel.co.il

Caterers
Hekelman: 02-532-2319
Aharonstein: 02-538-4534
Shalom Katz: 02-651-9096
Food Masters Metzger: 02-651-8255
Of Nof Ben Zion Meyers: 02-652-3247 or 02-651-9821
Erlichman Caterers: 02-651-9260
Dov Chaitowitz Catering: 02-651-9073
Choice Caterers: 02-651-0496
Shaarei Simcha: 02-500-1253
Hillary Morris: 02-993-2043

Flowers
Prachei Yerushalaim: 02-537-2666
Gila Parchi Gemach: 02-651-9958
Esther Miller: 02-537-3226
Rivka Eisenberg: 02-534-5501

Kesubot
Ready Made Artistic Kesuba Zeesi's Gifts: 02-652-5717
Faigie Perkal graphic artist, artistic, hand-written kesuba: 02-572-5336
Sarah Tikvah Kornbluth custom kesubas, painted or cut outs: tikvaket @netvision.net.il, 02-651-8442
Laurie Friedman graphic artist personal design and custom lettering: 02-534-5382

Photographers
Chaim Mayersdorf: 02-652-5541
Ariel Ravisky: 02-586-4272
Golan: 02-643-1514
Shteltzer: 02-643-3364
Photo Sherut: 02-623-3750
Gould: 02-537-3638

Videographers
Shimon Glass: 02-537-6550
Golan: 02-643-1514
Simcha Vision: 02-653-5113
Yehoshua Weiss: 02-651-9262

Musicians
Aryeh Glazer: 03-579-5781
Amiram Dvir: 03-570-9056
Alan Freishtat: 02-651-8502
Ephraim Mendelsohn: 02-999-0853
Peretz Bernstein: 02-652-0224

Invitations and Benchers
Miriam Marcus: Har Nof, 02-651-8702
Simchonim: 02-570-6915, https://simchonim.co.il/
Rose Printing: Dfus Hashoshanim (Meah Shearim), 02-538-9968
Bookshbine: 02-537-0106
Old City Press: Har Nof, 02-651-4701 or 02-651-1529
Rashie Reichert: 02-999-6548
Shlomit Stander: 02-652-8626
Chessed V'emunah: 02-537-3716

Monograms
Faigie Perkal graphic artist for a special, personalized monogram on your invitations and benchers: 02-572-5336
Sarah Tikvah Kornblut personalized invitation and bencher logos: 02-651-8442, tikvaket@netvision.net.il

Shtick Gemachim
Sanhedria: 02-537-1108
Mekor Baruch: 02-500-1159
Romema: 02-538-9859

Miscellaneous
Balloon sculptures Leah Phaff: 02-533-4549

List of Shadchanim in Eretz Yisroel

Julie Joanes	juliejoanes@gmail.com	052-711-2178
Danielle Leiba	danielleleiba@gmail.com	053-235-6179
Susan Reuben (also dating coach)	msreuben@gmail.com	058-764-9256
Masha Fabian	mashafabian@gmail.com	054-844-3528
Ravi Shahar	ravishahar59@gmail.com	052-761-8151
Sara Salomon	salomon36@etrog.net.il	052-764-9031
Chani Greenblatt	chanigreen2@gmail.com	054-604-2550
Merissa Gross	mg@merissagross.com	(prefers e-mail)
Michal Vas	Michal@vas.name	054-263-0977
Sarah Kotylar	sarahkotlyar@gmail.com	058-326-1361
Steve Rapoport	bargersh@yahoo.com	02-534-1213
Raizi Steinberg	rayimahuvim1@gmail.com	058-415-3050
Sheindle Dovolsky	sdovolsky@gmail.com	052-533-5459
Debbi Jacob	mikedebbikids@yahoo.com	052-277-2134
Julie Hoch	juliehoch120@gmail.com	02-651-8917
Avraham Ellis	Telegemach@gmail.com	053-315-9587
Aviva Trope	tropaviva528@gmail.com	052-762-9950
Chevy Weiss	https://theshadchanit.com/	
Miriam Lewitan	029992674l@gmail.com	

Made in the USA
Middletown, DE
27 October 2023